Say That Again

Words with Double Meanings in Nature

Michael J. Larson

Illustrated by Janine Ringdahl Schmidt

DORRANCE
PUBLISHING CO
EST. 1920
PITTSBURGH, PENNSYLVANIA 15238

The contents of this work, including, but not limited to, the accuracy of events, people, and places depicted; opinions expressed; permission to use previously published materials included; and any advice given or actions advocated are solely the responsibility of the author, who assumes all liability for said work and indemnifies the publisher against any claims stemming from publication of the work.

All Rights Reserved
Copyright © 2023 by Michael J. Larson

No part of this book may be reproduced or transmitted, downloaded, distributed, reverse engineered, or stored in or introduced into any information storage and retrieval system, in any form or by any means, including photocopying and recording, whether electronic or mechanical, now known or hereinafter invented without permission in writing from the publisher.

Dorrance Publishing Co
585 Alpha Drive
Pittsburgh, PA 15238
Visit our website at *www.dorrancebookstore.com*

ISBN: 979-8-88812-263-1
eISBN: 979-8-88812-763-6

Words in nature are not always clear;
Double meanings exist with some of the words
that we hear.
In this book, read words that are names for living
creatures,
And their double meanings will bring smiles to
students and even the teachers.

The Yellow Jacket

The first words on our list can be washed and dried;

Hanging on the clothesline, the bright yellow is seen far and wide.

During cold days you'll want to wear it to keep warm.

A yellow jacket I'm describing, worn in the city or on the farm.

The Yellow Jacket

Nature's 'Yellow Jacket' is a very busy little bug,
Buzzing the soda pop you're trying to "chug-a-lug".
Tree sap, flower nectar and fruits are also their thing,
But do not pester them or they may give you a sting!

The Dandy Lion

A 'dandy' lion may look really great;

With tuxedo and top hat he looks first rate!

But come on, kids, we know that's not true.

Try dressing a lion like that and he'd eat me and you!

The Dandelion

In nature, however, there is a 'dandelion' plant.

Its yellow flower has caused gardeners to rave and to rant!

But insects gather to feed on its blossoms so yellow,

And naturalists say its green leaves make a salad so mellow.

Horseshoe (crab)

The horseshoe 'clanked' as it hit the stake.

A second horseshoe plopped down and a ringer it did make!

After a day of throws, bangs, clunks and grabs,

All horseshoes must surely become 'horseshoe crabs'!

The Horseshoe Crab

Out in the ocean water close in by the shore,
Live the horseshoe crabs amid the crashing waves and roar.
In the shallow water, it crawls and digs in the sand.
As the tide comes and goes, their home changes from
        deep water to dry land.

The Dragon Fly!

If knights of old wanted to become real cool,
They'd slay a fire-breathing dragon using a sword
        as their only tool!
It's lucky dragons didn't have wings in those days gone by,
'Cause any knight chasing a dragon would watch the 'dragonfly'!

The Dragonfly

If you were a knight today you'd leave your sword at home,
Take a walk around a pond and see a real dragonfly roam.
They dart, dive and hover in the sky,
And when they get hungry they catch a mosquito on the fly!

Daddy's Long Legs

If your Daddy plays for the NBA or is a volleyball pro,

His childhood years were spent doing one thing…..

    grow, grow grow!

And now that you have become his child from your friends

    come many begs,

Take us to a game where we can watch your Daddy's long legs!

Daddy-long-legs

Daddy-long-legs exist and live in our great outdoors,
And children respond to them with screams and roars!
Many call them spiders but spiders they are not,
And over this fact many students have fought!

The Brown Bat

It makes a great birthday gift, the big brown bat.
On the diamond you can hit baseballs…splat, splat, splat!
Choose up sides one-by-one,
And put in nine innings of baseball fun!

The Brown Bat

Big brown bats are found in nature too,
Flying at night they capture insects to chew.
The only mammal that moves by flight,
Their leathery, flapping wings create a scary sight!

Letters A, D and J?

What if alphabet letters were colored too?

The A's were red, the D's yellow and the J's were blue.

When we read a book what a colorful sight,

Every bedtime story would be a rainbow of delight!

The Blue Jay

There is a Blue Jay in our outdoor world,

A bird resembling a blue, white and black banner unfurled.

When alarmed, it gives a harsh, loud cry.

It's the boss of the other birds 'cause it's not shy!

Butter Fly!

One morning I was preparing to eat a pancake stack;
I poured on maple syrup and my lips went "smack"!
Next you won't believe what I'm going to say,
As I reached for the butter the 'butterfly' away!

Butterflies

To see the butter fly in our house is a shock,
But we see them often in our garden and on our dock.
Their colorful patterns make a dazzling display,
But when we try to get a closer look the butterflies
always never stay!

Shoveler

Winter comes and the snow falls down;
Ten inches of the white stuff covers the town.
It's time to clean sidewalks, driveways and streets.
"Shovelers" are called upon to accomplish these feats!

Shoveler Duck

"Shovelers" are also found in our ponds and sloughs,
A large-billed duck that is fond of pond bottom 'ooze'!
Because its bill is large for straining food,
You can also call it a Spoonbill and not be considered rude!

Common Turn

If someone asked you to show them a common turn,
You'd probably laugh and think that's
 what we go to school to learn!
There's a right turn, a left turn…let's see, there should be one more.
Oh, yes, it's the U-turn that allows us to go where we
        have been before!

Common Tern

I'm sorry, I'm sorry, I wasn't clear,
Show me a common 'tern' is what I meant you to hear.
A tern is a bird with a deeply forked tail,
That hovers and dives into lakes where we sail.

Corn

I had a corn upon my toe;

The pain I thought would never go!

My 'tennies' became way too tight,

Bare feet in my sandals were an ugly sight.

Acorn

And then I heard and it came as a surprise,
Deer, squirrels and turkeys are acorn guys.
"A corn" and "acorn" are not the same you say?
Then it isn't possible that these animals could eat my corn away?

Cat

I've seen many cats in my day,

And each is made in the very same way.

Behind them is something that will twitch and flail,

And it is always referred to as a 'cat tail'.

Cattail

Along our pond edges and in the marsh,

Grow plants that prevent winds from becoming too harsh.

Food for muskrats and nesting sights for birds,

With all of these cattails not one "meow" can be heard!

Review Time!

So we have a final reminder before we stop,

Don't let "double meanings" make you feel like a nature flop!

Remember a "yellow jacket" can be something to wear,

But if it has wings and a stinger take care!

You might see a "dandy lion" in a cartoon,

But your dad sprays "dandelions" during May and June.

When you play "horseshoes" be careful what you grab,

If you use an ocean animal you might hear a "horseshoe crab" crab!

There is no danger that "dragons" will "fly",

But along pond edges we see a "dragonfly" mount to the sky!

"Daddy-long-legs" may help him 'slam-dunk',

But I've seen this creature scrambling up a tree trunk.

Using a "big brown bat" I hit a ball out of the park;

Later on a "big brown bat" scared me in the dark!

Paint the alphabet letters and make a "blue J",
Walk out into the garden and see it fly away!
During a cafeteria food fight you may see the "butterfly";
Travel to a city park and see them fill the sky.

You have been a "shoveler" when playing in the sand;
"Shovelers" swim among the mallards looking very grand!
Your mom took a "common turn" while driving you to school;
I watched a "common tern" in flight and thought it was so cool!

An "acorn" in your shoe is better than an "a corn" on the toe,
When you want it to leave it's not hard to make an "acorn" go!
A "cat tail" is on the end of your kitty,
But it's also a plant, narrow leafed and pretty.

So there are some words that may cause you to say,
"Excuse me, but say that again, and do it right away!"
Double meaning words may cause you to fret,
But you can still enjoy the outdoors and that's a sure bet!

www.ingramcontent.com/pod-product-compliance
Lightning Source LLC
Chambersburg PA
CBHW040904110726
48005CB00001B/188

9798888122631